I Wonder Why

Romans Wore Togas

and Other Questions About Ancient Rome

Fiona Macdonald

KINGFISHER

KINGFISHER
Kingfisher Publications Plc
New Penderel House
283–288 High Holborn
London WC1V 7HZ
www.kingfisherpub.com

First published by Kingfisher Publications Plc 1997
(hb) 10 9 8 7 6 5 4 3 2 1
(pb) 10 9 8
BS/0802/TIMS/UNV/113 MA
Copyright © Kingfisher Publications Plc 1997

A CIP catalogue record for this book is
available from the British Library

ISBN 0 7534 0119 3 (hb)
      0 7534 0148 7 (pb)

Phototypeset by Tradespools Ltd, Frome, Somerset

Printed in China

Series editor: Clare Oliver
Series designer: David West Children's Books
Author: Fiona Macdonald
Consultant: Dr Paul Roberts
Editor: Claire Llewellyn
Art editor: Christina Fraser
Picture researcher: Amanda Francis
Illustrations: Simone Boni (Virgil Pomfret) 16–17;
   Peter Dennis (Linda Rogers) 8–9, 28–29; Luigi Galante
   (Virgil Pomfret) 4–5, 18–19, 26–27; Christian Hook
   22–23, 30–31; Tony Kenyon (BL Kearley) all cartoons;
   Nicki Palin cover, 6–7, 14–15, 24–25; Claudia Saraceni
   12–13; Rob Shone 30bl; Thomas Trojer 20–21;
   David Wright (Kathy Jakeman) 10–11.

CONTENTS

4 Who were the Romans?

5 Did all the Romans live in Rome?

6 Who ruled Rome?

7 Who was born free?

7 Who slaved away for the Romans?

8 When did the army use tortoises?

9 Which soldiers left home for 25 years?

10 Who attacked the Romans with elephants?

11 Which Roman guards went quack-quack-quack?

11 Who cut the Romans to pieces?

12 Who did the Romans worship?

14 Why did Roman women look pale?

15 Why did Romans hit their hairdressers?

15 Why did Romans wear togas?

16 Why did Romans jump in the bath together?

17 How many people could fit on the loo?

18 Who lived in high-rise flats?

19 Which houses had holes in the roof?

19 Which guard dog was made of stone?

20 Who brought slaves, spices and silk?

21 Where was the world's first shopping centre?

22 Did the Romans eat pizza?

23 Why did people throw up at banquets?

23 Who ate lying down?

24 Who went to school in Roman times?

24 What language did the Romans speak?

25 What did the children play with?

26 Why were Roman roads so straight?

27 Which bridges were always full of water?

28 Who was thrown to the lions?

29 Were there hippos in the hippodrome?

30 Where can you visit a Roman town?

31 How do we know about the Romans?

32 Index

Who were the Romans?

The Romans were people who came from Rome. About 2,000 years ago they became so powerful that they began to conquer the lands around them. By AD100 they ruled a huge empire, and were one of the mightiest peoples in the ancient world.

● Different parts of the empire had very different climates. Romans boiled in Egypt, where the summers were sweltering...

● An old legend says that the city of Rome was first started by a man called Romulus. He and his twin brother Remus had been abandoned by their parents and looked after by a wolf!

Did all the Romans live in Rome?

- ...but they shivered in the icy Swiss Alps and in northern Britain. These were the coldest places in the whole empire.

The city of Rome wasn't big enough for all the Romans! All in all, there were about 50 million people in the empire, which stretched from Britain in the north to Africa in the south. Everyone in the empire was protected by Rome's armies, but had to obey Rome's laws.

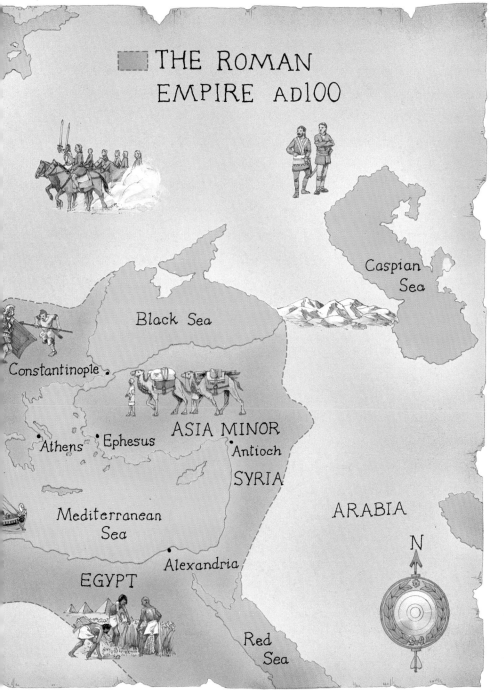

THE ROMAN EMPIRE AD100

Caspian Sea

Black Sea

Constantinople

Athens · Ephesus

ASIA MINOR

Antioch

SYRIA

Mediterranean Sea

ARABIA

N

Alexandria

EGYPT

Red Sea

3,000 miles

- It would have taken nearly 100 days to ride from one end of the empire to the other. It was a journey of over 3,000 Roman miles, about 5,000 kilometres.

Who ruled Rome?

Over the years, Rome was ruled in three different ways: first by kings, then by a number of officials who were chosen by the people, and finally by emperors, who were really kings under a different name!

● Some Roman emperors ruled wisely, but others did whatever they pleased…

Nero was mad and bad. Some people say he set fire to the city of Rome.

Hadrian visited every corner of the empire, and made it stronger.

Caligula wasted the riches of Rome. He believed he was a god.

Who was born free?

Roman citizens. They were not only able to vote in elections, they also got free seats at the amphitheatre and free use of the public baths. When times were hard, they got free loaves of bread, too!

● Roman women did not have the same rights as men. They were not allowed to vote, and had to obey their husband or father. But that doesn't mean they always did!

Who slaved away for the Romans?

Most of the hard work in Rome was done by slaves. These men, women and children were captured abroad, and then sold in the marketplace in Rome. They had to wear an identity tag with their master's name and address on it – just in case they got lost.

● The first Roman emperor was called Augustus. He was advised by a group of wealthy men, called senators, who were used to running the army and the government.

● Slaves were sometimes given their freedom after many years of good service, or if their master wanted to be kind.

When did the army use tortoises?

When Roman soldiers were advancing towards the enemy, they did a special trick called 'the tortoise'. They held their shields high above their heads to make a sort of shell. This protected them from enemy spears – but made it hard for them to see where they were going!

Dear Mum
iv/vii/civ
Having an awful time.
The Barbarians are fierce
and I think the Centurion
hates me.
Please send V sesterces
for food.
Your loving son
Marcus xxx

● Soldiers were often hungry and cold. Many of them wrote letters home asking for extra food and clothing.

● Injured soldiers bandaged their wounds with cobwebs soaked in vinegar. This helped the soldiers, but wasn't so good for the spiders!

Which soldiers left home for 25 years?

Most soldiers had to stay in the army for 25 years. Those who were Roman citizens were luckier – they could leave after just 20 years! Soldiers had a hard life. They were far from home, and had to put up with danger, tough training and harsh punishments.

Metal breastplate

Helmet

Spear

Pack and food

Dagger

Shield

Axe

Sword

Leather pad for protection

Woollen tunic

Leather sandals

● In warmer parts of the empire, soldiers didn't wear much under their tunics. But in chilly places they wore thick woollen underpants – just like the locals.

Who attacked the Romans with elephants?

Hannibal was the Spanish leader of the Carthaginians, a people from North Africa. He led a huge army and a herd of elephants across France and over the snow-covered Alps on a long march to Italy. In battle, the elephants charged at the Roman soldiers, who soon ran away in terror.

● Queen Cleopatra of Egypt used her beauty and charm to fight against the Romans. She made two Roman commanders fall in love with her – Julius Caesar and Mark Antony.

● In Britain the Romans built Hadrian's Wall, which was 120 kilometres long. From its towers, they spied on tribes in Scotland to the north.

- Forty thousand men and 37 elephants made the long, dangerous march from Spain across the Alps – the mountains in northern Italy. Sadly, many of them died from cold along the way.

Which Roman guards went quack-quack-quack?

A flock of holy geese lived among the temples on Rome's Capitoline Hill. One dark night, a fierce tribe called the Gauls were planning an attack. They crept up the hill, but were heard by the geese, who quacked a loud warning and saved the citizens of Rome.

Who cut the Romans to pieces?

When the Romans attacked Britain, they had to face fierce warriors like Queen Boudicca. Legend says she fixed sharp knives to the wheels of her chariot and then drove right into the lines of soldiers. Ouch!

Who did the Romans worship?

The Romans worshipped hundreds of different gods and goddesses. They believed that the gods watched over them night and day. Some looked after the earth and the sea. Some cared for special groups such as doctors, merchants or soldiers. And others watched over the different parts of people's lives – their health, beauty or love life.

Jupiter, king of the gods

● The Romans thought that snakes brought good luck, so they painted them on their walls.

Mars, god of war

● The Romans believed that spirits lived in the rivers, woods and fields. They protected wild animals and the plants that grew there.

Venus, goddess of love

12

Juno, queen of the gods

● Sick Romans prayed to the gods to cure them. If they got better, they left a thank-you present in the temple – a little statue of the part of their body that had been cured.

Neptune, god of the sea

Diana, goddess of the Moon and of hunting

Apollo, god of the Sun and of the arts

● The Romans built temples as homes for the gods. Each god or goddess had a temple of their own. It was built in the finest stone, and decorated with statues and carvings.

Why did Roman women look pale?

Pale skin was a sure sign that a woman came from a rich, noble family. Poorer women had to work outside. Their faces burnt in the hot summer sun, and became rough and red in the cold winter winds.

● Slaves mixed skin creams from all sorts of ingredients – such as flour, chalk, lead and asses' milk.

● Fashionable men wore perfume and make-up. They even had stick-on leather patches to hide any spots or scars.

● The Romans used all sorts of beauty tools – combs and hairpins made of bone, heated curling tongs, tweezers to pluck out stray hairs, and tiny spoons to scoop the wax from their ears.

Why did Romans hit their hairdressers?

Most Roman noblewomen had two or three slave girls to do their hair. Some of the women were cruel. They jabbed their slaves with a hairpin if the girls tugged their hair – and even whipped them if the style came out wrong.

● Wigs were very fashionable. Blonde hair came from German slaves. Dark glossy hair was bought from poor women in India.

Why did Romans wear togas?

Men wore togas for special ceremonies. Wearing one showed that you were a Roman citizen. Slaves weren't allowed to wear one. An ordinary citizen had a plain white toga, a senator's had a purple trim, while the emperor's was purple all over.

Why did Romans jump in the bath together?

In Roman times, baths weren't just places to get clean. They were more like today's health clubs. People went there to keep fit, play games or sports, meet up with their friends, relax after a hard day's work – and give themselves a jolly good wash, too!

● The Romans hardly ever used soap – but they weren't dirty. They rubbed olive oil all over their skin, and then scraped it off with a blunt metal tool called a strigil. The dirt on their skin came off with the oil.

● Hot air from underground furnaces was used to heat the bath water. But it also made the bottom of the bath very hot, so some people wore sandals rather than burn their feet!

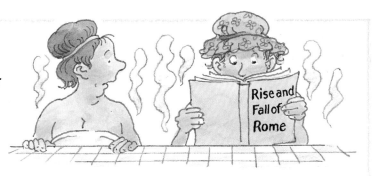

● Some public baths had a library – very handy for people who liked reading in the bath.

How many people could fit on the loo?

The Romans didn't go to the toilet on their own. Sometimes as many as 16 people sat side by side, laughing and chatting with one another. All of the cities had multi-seat public toilets. They were cheap to build, and easy to clean.

● Most homes didn't have a toilet. Families used big pottery jars instead.

Who lived in high-rise flats?

Rome was a crowded city, and short of space. Most ordinary people lived in blocks of flats about six storeys high. On the ground floor were noisy shops and taverns. At the top were stuffy attic rooms. The nicest flats were somewhere in between.

● The Romans liked gardening. Rich people's gardens had pools and fountains. But even the poorest families kept flowerpots on the windowsill.

● Roman high-rises were so badly built that they often fell down. To stop the accidents, the Emperor Augustus passed a law forbidding any new building more than 20 metres high.

Which houses had holes in the roof?

Rich people's houses were built around an open-air courtyard. The open roof let in daylight and cool breezes during the summer – but chilly wind and rain in the winter.

Which guard dog was made of stone?

Many Roman homes had a picture of a guard dog near the front door. Like all mosaics, they were made of tiny pieces of stone. The words 'CAVE CANEM' (say *cah-vay cah-nem*) meant 'Beware of the dog' – to scare off any burglars!

Who brought slaves, spices and silk?

Merchants travelled to the very ends of the empire, and beyond, to bring back goods for the citizens of Rome.

As well as ordinary things like corn and timber, they brought slaves from North Africa, spices from India and beautiful silk from China.

● Ostia was the port of Rome. It lay on the coast, 25 kilometres from the city. Sacks of corn and jars of wine and olive oil were stored in warehouses at the port, and sent up to the market by barge.

● Most merchants preferred to keep their ships in port all winter, safe from storms and shipwrecks.

● To prevent traffic jams, traders and farmers could only bring their goods into Rome at night. With all those noisy carts, it must have been hard to sleep!

Where was the world's first shopping centre?

Trajan's Forum was a marketplace in Rome's city centre. It had 150 shops, brand new offices, and a huge open space where traders could set up their stalls. Citizens strolled around the Forum, looking at the goods and gossiping with their family and friends.

Did the Romans eat pizza?

Every day the Romans bought hot pies and tasty treats, a bit like modern pizzas, from the eating-houses and taverns in the busy towns. The 'pizzas' were topped with onions, fish and olives – but not tomatoes, which were brought over from South America about 1,500 years later.

● The taverns did a roaring trade selling hot food and drink. Few families had a kitchen at home, and ovens were forbidden in high-rise flats, for fear of fire.

● In hot weather, rich people cooled their drinks with snow. It was carried down from the mountains by slaves.

Why did people throw up at banquets?

At the best banquets, many guests didn't have room for all the wonderful food and drink. To solve the problem, they'd sometimes go outside and make themselves sick. Then they returned to the table to eat some more!

● Wealthy Romans ate all sorts of fancy foods, such as boiled ostrich, or dormice in honey. They also liked surprises. At one banquet, a roast pig was carved open, and a flock of live thrushes flew out!

Who ate lying down?

Wealthy Romans didn't sit up at a table. Instead, they lay propped up on their elbows on long wooden couches. This must have given them indigestion. Their children had more sense – they sat on stools, close to their parents' couch.

Who went to school in Roman times?

● Roman children only studied three subjects at junior school – reading, writing and sums.

Boys and girls from well-off families went to school when they were seven years old. But poor children stayed at home. Some of them ran errands for their parents or looked for work. Others played in the street and got into trouble.

What language did the Romans speak?

Everyone who lived in Italy spoke Latin. Everywhere else in the empire, people spoke their own local languages. But there were so many that people from different parts of the empire had to learn Latin, too, so that they could all understand one another!

****

?????

24

• Girls left school at 11 but boys stayed on till they were 16 or 18 years old.

What did the children play with?

Roman children played with all sorts of odds and ends. If they couldn't afford glass or pottery marbles, they used little round nuts instead. They also threw dice made of bones. They even used pigs' bladders – blown up like balloons – to play football with!

CAESAR HORRIBILISSIMUS EST

• The Romans loved to scribble on walls. On many of their buildings you can still see the rude things they wrote about their leaders, enemies, and even their friends!

• The Romans used letters for numbers: I was 1, V was 5, X was 10, L was 50, and so on. Have you noticed the Roman page numbers in this book?

I, II, III, IV, V, VI, VII, VIII, IX, X, XI, XII, XIII, XIV...

Why were Roman roads so straight?

The Romans were brilliant engineers. Before they built a road, they used measuring instruments to work out where the road should go. They chose the shortest, straightest route between two camps, forts, or towns – and got rid of any hedges, buildings or other obstacles in the way. The roads linked the whole empire.

PLAN VIEW

SIDE ELEVATION

ARCHITECT
Marcu

● Road-builders put milestones along the side of the road so that travellers knew how far they had gone. A Roman mile was 1,000 paces long, about 1.6 kilometres.

ROME
500
MILES

● The roads had strong foundations. On the bottom, a thick layer of sand was covered first by stones, and then by gravel. On the top was a smooth surface of carefully-fitted paving stones.

Which bridges were always full of water?

Aqueducts look rather like bridges, but instead of a pathway along the top they have a deep channel of water. The Romans built them to carry water from mountain streams to nearby cities. Without aqueducts, the people wouldn't have had their baths, toilets or fountains of fresh running water.

● The Romans invented arches, too. Each arch rested on a wooden frame until the very last stone, called the keystone, was in place.

● The Romans invented concrete by mixing lime, water and the ash from volcanoes. Concrete was as strong as stone, and it set hard even under water.

Who was thrown to the lions?

● The amphitheatre in Rome was the Colosseum. It could seat up to 50,000 spectators.

On special days, people flocked to see spectacular shows at the amphitheatre. Christians, criminals and slaves were thrown into a ring with lions, and were chased, wounded and killed. The crowds cheered noisily. They thought it was fun to watch people suffer – but to us it seems wicked and cruel.

● Watching men fight was another popular sport. Gladiators were slaves who were sent into the arena to kill animals – or each other – to please the bloodthirsty crowds.

- Lions, leopards, crocodiles, wolves and bears – many different kinds of animal were shipped to Rome from all over the empire. Thousands were killed in the amphitheatre in a single day.

Were there hippos in the hippodrome?

The hippodrome, or circus, was a huge sports stadium with an oval-shaped racetrack. There were no hippos, but there were exciting chariot races. This was the Romans' favourite sport, and huge crowds filled the hippodrome to bet on their favourite teams.

Where can you visit a Roman town?

Pompeii was a bustling town not far from Rome. In the year AD 79, a nearby volcano erupted, and buried the town in ash. Pompeii lay hidden for centuries until, one day, some farmers discovered its Roman remains. Today you can visit to see what life was like in Roman times.

• Archaeologists have studied Pompeii since the 1800s, and have uncovered an almost-perfect Roman town.

MAKING MODELS

1 People were buried by the volcano's ash. Over the years, their bodies rotted away, leaving people-shaped holes in the hardened ash, or rock.

2 Archaeologists used the holes as moulds. They poured plaster inside, and waited for it to set.

3 Chipping away at the rock left plaster models of the Romans. Archaeologists study these carefully to learn about Roman life.

● Mount Vesuvius was an active volcano. As it erupted, showers of ash poured onto Pompeii, killing the people with poisonous fumes.

● The Roman empire grew weaker and weaker. It was attacked by warriors from the north and the east, who split up the empire into many small kingdoms.

How do we know about the Romans?

The Roman empire came to an end in the 470s. Yet Roman buildings, mosaics, writings, paintings and weapons have all survived. Remains like these tell us about the people and the way they lived.

● Some Roman finds are rather peculiar. Archaeologists in London have dug up a pair of black leather knickers. Who could have lost them all those years ago?

Index

A

Africa 4, 5, 10, 20
Alps 4, 5, 10, 11
amphitheatre 7, 28-29
Apollo 13
aqueduct 27
archaeologist 30, 31
army 5, 7, 8-9, 10, 11, 12
Augustus 7, 18

B

banquet 23
baths 7, 16-17, 27
Britain 4, 5, 10, 11
Boudicca 11
building 18, 26-27, 31

C

Caligula 6
Capitoline Hill 11
Carthage 4, 10
chariot 11, 29
circus see hippodrome
citizen 7, 9, 15
Cleopatra 10
clothing 8, 9, 15
Colosseum 28

D

Diana 13

E

Egypt 4, 5, 10
emperor 6, 7, 15

F

flat 18, 22
food 8, 9, 22-23

G

Gaul 4, 11
gladiator 28
god 6, 12-13

H

Hadrian 6
Hadrian's Wall 4, 10-11
Hannibal 10-11
hippodrome 29

J

Juno 13
Jupiter 12

K

keystone 27

L

Latin 24

M

make-up 14
marketplace 7, 20, 21
Mars 12
merchant 12, 20
milestone 26

N

Neptune 13
Nero 6
number 25

P

Pompeii 4, 30-31
port 20

R

road 26-27
Roman empire 4-5, 6, 9, 20, 24, 26, 29, 31
Rome, city of 4, 5, 6, 18, 20, 21, 28

S

school 24, 25
senator 7, 15
ship 20

shop 18, 21
slave 7, 14, 15, 20, 22, 28
soldier see army
strigil 16

T

tavern 18, 22
temple 11, 13
toga 15
toilet 17, 27
toy 25
trade 20-21

V

Venus 12
Vesuvius 31

W

wig 15